.50

p 42 has _____
wds × 94 pp
⟶ 300
30,000
3   wds
at most

Contraception and Catholics

CONTRACEPTION
and CATHOLICS:

a new appraisal

by

LOUIS DUPRÉ, L.S.T., Ph.D.

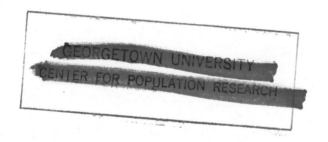

HELICON
Baltimore-Dublin

Helicon Press, Inc.
1120 N. Calvert Street
Baltimore, Maryland 21202

Library of Congress Catalog Card Number 64-23614

PRINTED IN THE UNITED STATES OF AMERICA BY
GARAMOND/PRIDEMARK PRESS, BALTIMORE, MD.

Preface

The purpose of this analysis is to contribute to a long overdue discussion of the arguments which Catholics usually propose against the use of artificial birth control under any circumstances. Since an argument always involves a process of reasoning by which a conclusion is drawn from particular propositions, there is no reason why the argument should not be open to a frank and honest discussion. The outcome of this study is admittedly rather negative: like the plague-stricken animals of La Fontaine,[1] even those arguments which do not die, prove to be somewhat sick. However, the inconclusiveness of the existing "proofs" does not settle the issue. For a Roman Catholic, the Church has a teaching authority in morals as well as in matters of faith. It is this authority that will give the ultimate answer to the question which so occupies us today. Yet, it would seem that the Church has not yet given such an answer, and this makes a critical discussion of the arguments *pro* and *contra* all the more urgent. As

1. "Ils ne mouraient pas tous, mais tous étaient frappés," "Les animaux malades de la peste," *Fables*.

a Catholic, I wish to state explicitly that whatever the magisterium's final word on the question will be, it will also be mine.

At the end of this study my thanks go to the *Georgetown Center for Population Research* for having helped me in so many ways, to Father John McLaughlin, S.J. for his constant support and encouragement, and to many others, most of all to those who did not share my views and yet were generous enough to provide me with essential information. It is obvious that I alone am responsible for the ideas here expressed. Grateful acknowledgement is made to *Cross Currents* and *The Commonweal* for permission to republish parts of this book which first appeared as articles.

Contents

Contents

Contraception and Catholics

Introduction

Few problems in this century have caused as much commotion in the Catholic Church as the problem of birth control. The Church's position on this subject has been a stumbling block for Catholics and non-Catholics alike. This in itself is nothing to be alarmed about. The Church has never been timorous of embracing unpopular causes—and much to her credit, for her foresight and resolution in the moral sphere have steadily directed the Western conscience towards greater awareness of the unique value of the human person.

We often forget that the humanitarianism of which our civilization is so proud today was first established by the Church in a centuries-long struggle against barbarism and obscurantism. Even though in worldly dealings Church authorities have not always cringed from the use of physical force to assert their policies, we must admit that the long, historical evolution towards respect for human dignity and personal integrity finds its source and constant support in the Church's steadfast insistence on Christian principles.

And these principles, even today, are far from popular, as is manifest in the widespread resistance to the Church's stand on racial equality. We are all aware of the deficiencies of many Catholics, including members of the hierarchy, in this respect, but the simple fact remains that ever since the epistles of St. Paul there has been no room in Christianity for a distinction between "Greeks and non-Greeks."

Yet, in most such conflicts, there has been a clearly defined point of Christian doctrine at issue, whereas the scriptural and traditional foundations of the commonly taught position on birth control are much harder to locate. The problem that we are facing today is new: it did not exist even at the beginning of the century, as a recognized problem. Therefore, the Church should not be reproved for failing to provide an immediate solution. In addition, the problematic situation itself changes from day to day, for new technical developments continually alter its conditions and circumstances. The theological publications on the subject, which are appearing at an ever increasing pace, show that Catholic moralists are not lacking in industry or courageous thinking. But if courage and clearheadedness are needed on the part of the theologians, some patience and confidence seem to be required from the faithful.

One must not forget that some of the most basic values of human existence are at stake. We should not blame the Church for being extremely prudent, for it is her wont not to deal lightly with the life whose infinite value she has revealed and proclaimed. Although the controversy, by its nature, must evoke emotion, high passions cannot provide the solution. Theological matters are not decided by a popularity vote of Christians. The labels of "liberal" and "conservative" which are often attached to the defendents of opposing views may be useful in the political arena—in theology they are inappropriate, and can only cloud the issue.

It is necessary to make these introductory remarks because the following considerations are not intended as a call for "change." They merely constitute an attempt to situate the problem in the context of the Church's basic tradition, in order to find guidance for a solution in the present. Since the deposit of faith is to be found in Scripture and tradition, a truth in the Catholic Church can only be traditional—however "conservative" this may sound.

Yet, it is not always an easy task to find the "traditional" answer to a new problem. Sometimes it may require very serious rethinking of positions that have been uncritically, if widely, accepted over a number of years. To discover an authentic Christian position takes more than a mere repetition of what we have heard before—it may call for a revision of what theologians have simply taken for granted and never thought out.

The ultimate criteria in determining this position are Scripture and *the infallible* teaching authority of the Church. But to use these criteria we must know what the Bible teaches and what precisely the Church affirms in an infallible statement. This is by no means as easy as it is often believed to be and in some cases may require years of historical and philological research. To cite just one example: the condemnation of Peter John Olivi's theory of the threefold division of the soul, in the Council of Vienne (1311-12), gradually came to be considered by many theologians who had lost sight of the historical circumstances, as a formal and unconditional acceptance of Aristotle's psychology. In a letter to Msgr. Hautcoeur, Rector of the Catholic Institute of Lille, France, Pius IX finally declared that the intention of the Council was not to impose the Aristotelian system of matter and form—a conclusion which the theologians could have reached by themselves if they had paid attention to the fact that a great number of the Council Fathers held the very theories which later generations thought to be condemned by the Council.

In the first chapter we will see that Scripture and early tradition do not deal with our problem, and that the view of marriage in both the Old and the New Testament does not necessarily exclude the use of contraception. Most theologians opposing birth control would easily agree on this. To support their position they refer rather to the clear stand which ecclesiastical authorities have taken on the subject over the last forty years, and which was prepared by a centuries-old consensus among moral theologians. In the second chapter it will become clear that the statements so far made by the magisterium on this point are not to be understood as infallible and that although the principles which they enunciate are as true today as they were in the past, the situation to which these principles were applicable has changed so much that they are no longer the only ones to be considered.

Some theologians who admit that the Church has not used its infallible authority in this matter would still maintain that the Catholic position cannot be changed because it is based on the natural law. I would agree with them that the precept of procreation results from the natural law, but I doubt whether this precept necessarily applies to each individual act of intercourse. All too often the physical aspect of the act is detached from the moral intention in a way which makes morality degenerate into biologism. The fourth chapter shows that if one includes the intention in the total moral aspect of the marriage act, as theologians have done recently in their solutions of moral cases, the possibility of a different position exists. In a final chapter there is a brief discussion of the value and limitations of some psychological and phenomenological arguments which have been proposed over the last years as the natural law thesis came more and more under attack.

CHAPTER 1

Scripture and Early Tradition

With some recent studies at hand, we must first examine the teaching of the Scriptures, and its interpretation by the early theologians, on the end and meaning of marriage. An attentive reading of the Holy Scripture seems to shed some new light on a problem which until recently was always treated in terms of a rather dubious notion of natural law. Will the new approach lead to a different solution? It is impossible to answer this question at the present moment. But at least one moral theologian, Professor Louis Janssens of Louvain, finds substantial support for a new position in a comparison between St. Paul and the spurious interpretation of his doctrine by St. Augustine, which was at the origin of a new and more rigid tradition in marital ethics.[1]

However, before going into that, it is necessary to discuss briefly the one passage that may seem to be directly relevant to a discussion of contraception: the description of Onan's act and its punishment in Genesis 38: 8-10. Judah, the son of Jacob, had chosen a wife for his oldest son, Er, but Er died. Then Judah said

1. Louis Janssens, "Morale conjugale et progestogènes," *Ephemerides Theologicae Lovanienses*, December 1963, pp. 787-826.

to his second son, Onan: " 'Marry your brother's widow; do the duty of a brother-in-law to her, and rear a family for your brother.' But Onan, knowing that the family would not be his, wasted his semen on the ground whenever he had intercourse with his brother's widow, so as not to give his brother a family. What he did was so displeasing to the Lord that he killed him too."

Before explaining this text, let me remark that it is always dangerous to use the Old Testament as a criterion of Christian marital ethics, since the mores of the Patriarchs in this domain were so far removed from our present morality that even most non-Christians today follow stricter rules. Yet, in this case, the severity might seem to be on the side of the Old Testament. It therefore deserves careful analysis.

In what did Onan's sin consist? Three different answers have been given to this question. Some interpreters claim that it was the contraceptive act itself (regardless of the circumstances); others, the lack of charity toward his brother; still others, the violation of the levirate law by which a man had to marry his deceased brother's widow. In an authoritative study,[2] Father A. M. Dubarle, O.P., a well-known French exegete, reaches the following conclusion: the violation of the levirate law offers a sufficient explanation for Onan's punishment. Even if one grants that this law did not entail a heavy obligation, he points out, the levirate marriage, *once it had been accepted,* certainly implied a grave obligation to provide offspring for one's

2. Father A. M. Dubarle, O.P., "La Bible et les Pères ont-ils parlé de la contraception?" *Supplément de la vie spirituelle,* 1962, pp. 573-610.

brother's family. This, after all, was the only reason why the widow had to take her brother-in-law as husband, rather than a man of her own choosing. To accept the marital union, and yet refuse the obligations that alone justified it, constituted a serious sin against justice and honesty. Not the contraceptive act in itself, but this act in the peculiar context of the levirate law, is at stake. The Torah has explicit and minute regulations of sexual conduct, but it does not mention contraception, even though Onan's practice was common knowledge.

In the commentaries of the Fathers on this passage, no one before St. Augustine seems to have interpreted it as a condemnation of contraceptive practices. Nor, for that matter, is even one clear condemnation of such practices to be found. Father Dubarle's study is most revealing on this point. The *Didachè*, probably the oldest non-canonical Christian text (early 2nd century), does not mention contraception in its list of sexual sins, although abortion is mentioned. St. Clement of Alexandria (3rd century) and St. Ambrose (4th century), though they both give a great deal of attention to sexual matters, do not have one word on contraception.

In a few cases one might perhaps find an implicit condemnation of it, but even this remains doubtful. Lactantius (4th century), for example, sees no other alternative than complete continence for a man who is too poor to raise numerous children. St Jerome, a notorious woman-hater, describes with gusto and at length the frivolities of the young ladies of his day. One of the things he does not approve of is that "some take a sterilizing drink before (intercourse) and commit homicide on a man who is not even conceived." But even here it is impossible to decide whether he condemns the practice because of its contraceptive or of its abortive effect. Father Dubarle favors the second interpretation on the ground that the story of Onan is never mentioned in his commentaries on Genesis. Only with St. Augustine (4th-5th centuries) does the picture change altogether, both for the interpretation of Onan's act and for the clear condemnation of contraception. But to evaluate St. Augustine's views correctly it is necessary to place them in the context of his position on marriage. After we determine what the Bible says about the end and practice of marriage, we can then compare the two.

In Genesis we have two different versions of the origin of marriage, each of them emphasizing a different aspect. The first chapter of Genesis, which probably goes back to a more recent and more sophisticated source, simply states:

> So God created man in his own image; in the image of God he created him; he created both male and female. Then God blessed them, and God said to them: "Be fruitful, multiply, fill the earth and subdue it" (Gn 1:27-28).

The story of Genesis 2 is more anthropomorphic and probably also older:

> For man himself no helper was found who was like him. Then the Lord God had a trance fall upon the man; and when he had gone to sleep, he took one of his ribs, closing up its place with flesh. The rib which he took from the man the Lord God built up into a woman, and

brought her to the man, whereupon the man said,
"This at last is bone of my bone, and flesh of my flesh;
she shall be called woman, for from man was she taken."

And the sacred author adds a moral to his story for
any who might entertain doubt about its meaning:
"That is why a man leaves his father and mother, and
clings to his wife, so that they form one flesh" (Gn 2:20-
24). The meaning that he wants to communicate is
different from, or more correctly, complementary to
the one in the first chapter. In Genesis 2, the woman
is the companion of the man, made of his own body
and destined to return to it. The marital union is
described in psychological terms, whereas in the first
chapter only procreation was mentioned. In the rest
of the Old Testament the emphasis is primarily on the
procreative aspect of marriage, with the one notable
exception of the *Song of Songs* where all the attention
goes to the pleasant companionship of the two lovers.

In the New Testament, the procreative end of marriage is always implied. Yet, the advice which St. Paul
gives to married Christians does not explicitly refer to
it. Here is the main text: "It is a good thing for a man
to have nothing to do with women; but because there
is so much immorality, let each man have his own wife
and each woman her own husband. The husband must
give the wife what is due to her, and the wife equally
must give the husband his due. The wife cannot claim
her body as her own; it is her husband's. Equally, the
husband cannot claim his body as his own; it is his
wife's. Do not deny yourselves to one another, except
when you agree upon a temporary abstinence in order
to devote yourselves to prayer; afterwards you may

come together again; otherwise, for lack of self-control, you may be tempted by Satan" (1 Cor 7:1-5).

St. Paul makes it unmistakably clear, as does the entire New Testament, that ideally the state of virginity is superior to that of marriage. But for most Christians marriage is the *safer* solution. Old age only strengthened the Apostle's view on this point. While in 1 Corinthians 7:8 he still recommended young widows to remain celibate, and to marry only if they could not control themselves, in his later epistle to Timothy he writes: "It is my wish that young widows shall marry again, have children and preside over a home; then they will give no opponent occasion for slander. For there have in fact been widows who have taken the wrong turning and gone to the devil" (1 Tim 5:14-15). One almost has the impression that some bitter experiences with young widows have wisened the Apostle.

In all this, there is not much talk about love. But neither is there the fear of the flesh which becomes so predominant in later Christian theology. And Paul's prosaic advice sounds most refreshing when compared with St. Augustine's and the Scholastics' interpretation of it. Furthermore, if the quoted texts may seem to strike a negative note, in the Epistle to the Ephesians St. Paul attributes to marital love the highest religious meaning that any human relation can have.

> Husbands, love your wives, as Christ also loved the church and gave himself up for it, to consecrate it, cleansing it by water and word, so that he might present the church to himself all glorious, with no stain or wrinkle or anything of the sort, but holy and without

blemish. In the same way men also are bound to love their wives, as they love their own bodies. In loving his wife a man loves himself. For no one ever hated his own body: on the contrary, he provides and cares for it; and that is how Christ treats the church, because it is his body, of which we are living parts. Thus it is that (in the words of Scripture) 'a man shall leave his father and mother and shall be joined to his wife, and the two shall become a single body.' It is a great truth that is hidden here. I for my part refer it to Christ and to the church, but it applies also individually: each of you must love his wife as his very self; and the woman must see to it that she pays her husband all respect (Eph 5:25-33).

What greater praise of love can anyone expect? And it is to be noted that Paul does not deal exclusively with spiritual love. There is an explicit reference to the body, which is even confirmed by the citation of Genesis 2.

After this beautiful text on the sense of love in Christian marriage, the writings of St. Augustine on marital ethics make rather distressing reading. One can hardly escape the impression that, with him, the theology of marriage got on the wrong track and stayed there for many centuries. Neo-Platonism and Gnosticism (mostly of the Manichean type) seem to have had as much impact on this theology as the ideas of the New Testament. To be sure, dualistic and spiritualistic views, in which only the spiritual world is good and the material world (including sex and marriage) evil, were at work long before the beginning of Christianity: the Fourth Gospel, with its emphasis on the Logos which has become flesh, was probably written to refute a particular form of Gnostic dualism. Yet, this dualism was never given official recognition during the first ages of Christianity, and often ended up in some dead-end street of heresy. Through St. Augustine's writings, however, it gained status and was accepted in respectable Christian theology. And it has retained its force right up to today, due to the enormous prestige of the Father of Latin theology.

In an important historical study, which was published after these pages were completed, Father Joseph E. Kerns, S.J., explains this development as follows:

> Once the Church had moved out of Palestine, all study and speculation took place in an ancient pagan culture which had an ingrained suspicion of matter and pleasure. Augustine not only grew up in this atmosphere but for several years was even a Manichaean. And his was the theology handed down to Western Europe. The Schoolmen received it hallowed by time, enhanced by the absence of any comparable body of thought since his death, and strengthened by a few spurious documents which gave it more official sanction than it really had. Blending with the Graeco-Roman concept of man which they were discovering in the pages of Aristotle, it could not help but affect their view of what Christ had revealed.[3]

3. Joseph E. Kerns, *The Theology of Marriage,* Sheed and Ward, New York, 1964, p. 88. See also p. 49. As Father Kerns points out, in other respects the influence of Augustine on the theology of marriage has been beneficial, since he propagated the idea that marriage is an intrinsic good, against the opinion of some of the Greek Fathers for whom marriage was merely a result of original sin. Unfortunately, for Augustine, sexual desire after the Fall is always inordinate and does not participate in the goodness of marriage as a divine institution. At best, the desire can be redeemed by it. On this subject one may consult Joseph E. Kerns, *op. cit.,* pp. 35-37, 47.

One might think that at least the public *mores* would have profited from an austere, spiritualistic view of man, but certainly in the extreme instances (for which Augustine is not responsible), the opposite seems to be true. If man's sexual life belongs to a realm of evil and degradation, it becomes almost impossible to establish solid moral standards to govern it. Some men abandoned all norms, since total perversion does not allow any differentiation, as did some medieval forms of Manicheism; others erected norms so strict that heroism was required to abide by them, as did the Puritans and the Jansenists. The frantic emphasis on sex in the United States today is certainly in good part to be explained as a reaction against a puritan morality that makes sex all the more fascinating by declaring it evil.[4] But instead of focusing on these clearly heterodox forms of Christianity, it would be more profitable to have a look at the marital ethics of traditional Christian theology as guided by St. Augustine.

Comparing the texts of Scripture with St. Augustine's exegesis of them, one almost feels transposed into another world. The three aspects which St. Augustine sees in marriage are all in the Scripture: *proles* (offspring), *fides* (fidelity), *sacramentum* (sacred and symbolic pledge—Christian mystery),[5] but somehow the entire perspective has changed. They are not integrated, as in Scripture, on the same plane: marriage

4. This opinion is confirmed in Joseph E. Kerns, S.J., *op. cit.*, pp. 91-92.

5. It is very difficult to render the exact meaning of the word *sacramentum* in Augustine. The term seems to be flexible and varies with the context in which it is used. For the first meaning see: Joseph E. Kerns, S.J., *op. cit.*, p. 198.

as Christian mystery belongs entirely to a spiritual order which has nothing to do with sex. Sexual relations are permitted only in the light of the other two aspects: to provide offspring (*proles*), and to prevent adultery by one's partner (*fides*).[6] They do not contribute anything to the sacramental value of marriage. Actually, for the good of the sacramental aspect it would be much better if husband and wife could live in complete continence. This theory was so accepted in the Middle Ages that a great theologian in the Augustinian tradition, Hugh of St. Victor, could claim that the marriage contract does not *per se* include the right to sexual intercourse.

In his recent article in the *Ephemerides* of the theological faculty of Louvain, Canon Louis Janssens shows how St. Augustine reinterprets St. Paul's precepts for Christian marriage in the First Epistle to the Corinthians (1 Cor 7:1-7). Whereas for St. Paul, husband and wife have the full right over each other's bodies, St. Augustine restricts this right to the exclusive purpose of procreation. To claim one's marriage right when there is no need for procreation is a venial sin. This doctrine continued into medieval theology. For St. Thomas there are only two cases in which intercourse can be had without sin: in order to procreate, or to *give* one's partner his due when he or she claims it. Not before the seventeenth century was it admitted that sexual relations in which there was neither need nor hope for procreation could be *claimed* without sin.

In fact, St. Augustine's theory goes even further: all sexual pleasure and desire are intrinsically evil for him.

6. See: *De Nuptiis et Concupiscentia*, lib. 2, c. 21. *P.L.*, 44, 457.

Only the purpose of procreation and the intention of preserving one's partner's fidelity can convert this evil into a good by subjugating it to a moral end. Augustine's entire theory of original sin has been tinted by this strange, sexual pessimism. For him the essence of original sin is concupiscence, and it is transmitted to further generations through the sexual desire in the act of conception.[7] This doctrine remained prevalent in the Western Church until the eleventh century, when St. Anselm replaced it by his definition of original sin as guilty *absence* of original justice.

Professor Janssens attacks this spurious dualism between spiritual love and sexual procreation. Undoubtedly, marital love is spiritual, but it is distinguished from all other love by the sexual attraction between persons of the opposite sex. If marital love is to maintain its *specific* character, the *eros* must be included within the *agape*, the charity, between husband and wife. To express itself this love has at its disposal the total bodily surrender, symbol of the gift of one's entire person, of which St. Paul speaks. The subjective intention of love (the *finis operantis*), then, is no longer extrinsic to an act whose only objective meaning would be procreation. No, the desire to express love belongs as much to the *intrinsic* and *objective* meaning of the marital act (and not merely to the subjective intention of the agent), as the intention to create new life. In chapter four we will see to what far-reaching conclusions this may lead.

7. It should be repeated, however, that St. Augustine never considered *marriage itself* a result of original sin. He explicitly rejected this opinion and was convinced that marriage was instituted before the Fall. See: *Genesi ad Litteram*, lib. 9, cc. 3-5; 8, *P.L.*, 34, 394-5; 398.

CHAPTER 2

The Problem of Ecclesiastical Authority

Let us now examine whether the past condemnations of artificial birth control can claim the infallible authority of the Church, which some moralists have ascribed to it.

The strongest and most authoritative text is to be found in Pope Pius XI's encyclical, *Casti Connubii*:

> Since, therefore, openly departing from the uninterrupted Christian tradition, some recently have judged it possible solemnly to declare another doctrine regarding this question, the Catholic Church, to whom God has entrusted the defence of the integrity of morals, standing erect in the midst of the moral ruin which surrounds her, in order that she may preserve the chastity of the nuptial union from being defiled by this foul stain, raises her voice in token of her divine ambassadorship and through Our mouth proclaims anew: any use whatsoever of matrimony exercised in such a way that the act is deliberately frustrated in its natural power to generate life is an offence against the law of God and nature, and those who indulge in such are branded with the guilt of a great sin.

It would be dishonest to minimize the meaning or the intention of this statement. The only question which can be raised here is: is it infallible? The fact that the statement is made in an encyclical does not decide this question. Infallible statements are not restricted to any particular literary form. As one theologian puts it:

> Irrespective of how it is issued, the nature of the binding force of papal teaching depends primarily on the intention of its source. On this view it is clear that the teaching of encyclicals may or may not, according to the circumstances, be infallible. In other words, the Pope can use the medium of an encyclical for the purpose of making an extraordinary exercise of his teaching power. But it is quickly added that, as a general rule, this is not the way in which infallible statements are issued. Unless the contrary is proved, it must be generally assumed that the teaching of any part of any encyclical is not infallible, apart from what is a repetition of something that has already been issued in an *ex cathedra* statement.[1]

A few authoritative moral theologians (particularly F. Capello, S.J. and A. Vermeersch, S.J.) have taken Pope Pius XI's words to be a definition *ex cathedra* because of the solemnity of its expression. But most theologians do not agree with this opinion, and Father Vermeersch himself admits that the phrasing is somewhat unusual for a papal definition. To me, the very fact that there is so much doubt and disagreement on this most fundamental point, seems to settle the issue. A statement *ex cathedra* must eliminate all reasonable doubt as to whether it is made *ex cathedra*. This is obviously not the case in the present instance since

1. Jeremiah Newman, *Principles of Peace*, Faith Press, 1964, p. 4.

the great majority of theologians at least doubt it. Consequently, we may safely conclude that it is not *solemnly* defined (*de fide definita*) as a point of Christian doctrine.

Yet, the possibility remains that the doctrine would be infallible, not because of a solemn declaration but because it has been taught unanimously and explicitly over a long period of time under the ordinary teaching of the Church. Precisely because in his opinion the doctrine proposed by Pius XI has been constantly taught by the Holy See, the moral theologians, and the bishops of the major European countries, J. Creusen, S.J. considers it infallible.[2] Here again, however, there are major disagreements, particularly as to whether there has ever been a real tradition: both the ethical situation, and most of the proposed measures to cope with it, are new and did not exist in a relatively recent past. That the contemporary situation has given rise to fundamentally new problems is reflected in recent official documents and theological opinions on the end and practice of marriage. Father P. Pinxten, S.J. therefore concludes in an article in *De Tijd* (June 19, 1963), the leading Dutch Catholic newspaper:

> I deny the applicability of the criterion [that papal pronouncements and a general consensus of bishops, theologians and faithful have asserted this doctrine of morals over a long period of time] to the present doctrine. First, the consensus concerning this doctrine has

2. "L'onanisme conjugal," -I- "l'enseignement du Magistère ordinaire," in *Nouvelle Revue Théologique,* 559 (1932), pp. 132-142. For this whole discussion see: John C. Ford, S.J. and Gerald Kelly, S.J., *Contemporary Moral Theology, II– Marriage Questions,* Newman Press, 1963, pp. 263-271.

certainly not existed over a long time: it merely covers a period of a few decades, a fraction of the time in which the Church has existed. Further, one can hardly speak of "consensus" when a truly open discussion between theologians and other specialists in the field has never taken place, when the opinion of the bishops on this matter has never been requested and when there has never been question of consulting the most interested people—married laymen. In view of the byzantinism from which the ecclesiastical circles have suffered during recent decades more than ever before—and from which we begin to be freed by Pope John's and the Council's attitude—one must not be surprised that bishops and theologians knew better than to state a possibly dissenting opinion and that "the doubt which exists in large circles" only now begins to break out. It is, in my opinion, typical that this doubt after so many years of repression has already spread so rapidly and so widely. Consequently, on the basis of this criterion one can certainly not claim infallibility for the present doctrine.

However much I agree with the general import of Father Pinxten's words, his statement that the consensus on this doctrine "merely covers a period of a few decades" must be qualified. For at least "onanism" has been condemned by all moralists (to my knowledge) since St. Augustine. The recent practices to prevent conception can be said to avoid this condemnation only if it is proved *either* that they are essentially different from "onanism" *or* that certain factors which led in the past to a universal condemnation of "onanism" are not always present in the contemporary situation. As to the first point, there is indeed a clear difference between *coitus interruptus*, the practice generally known as "withdrawal," which has been condemned throughout the ages, and the present use of pill or diaphragm. Whereas the former could be considered as a form of masturbation, the latter does not exclude a full expression of marital love (even though it excludes procreation), and could therefore be said to respect at least one essential meaning of the marital act.

Yet, this distinction by no means settles the case, since moral theologians for several centuries have also condemned contraception in more general terms (not just *coitus interruptus*). St. Alphonsus writes:

> It is sinful to do anything during or after the marital act which would prevent conception or which would eject the conceived semen.[3]

Even more impressive is Cajetan's opinion, which in its precise and clear formulation condemns practices hundreds of years before their discovery. In marriage, he writes,

> [An act which prevents conception is a sin against nature, if it is accomplished by ejaculating outside the natural receptacle,] or if during ejaculation within the natural receptacle something is done to prevent conception, whether on the part of the man or on the part of the woman, regardless of the instrument or method which is used, since then the act of intercourse is deliberately frustrated from the attainment of its natural end.[4]

3. *Theologia Moralis*, Book VI, p. 954: "Peccant tamen [conjuges] si in usu matrimonii vel post usum faciant aliquid quo impediatur conceptio aut semen conceptum rejiciatur."
4. "Sive, seminando intra vas naturale, detur opera ut non sequatur conceptio, aut ex parte viri aut ex parte feminae, quacumque id arte vel industria fiat, quoniam tunc ex in-

Of course, the opinion of a private theologian is never decisive. Yet, what Cajetan, Busenbaum, Alphonsus and others write was accepted doctrine, even though it was not always as clearly formulated, and it certainly proves that the moral rejection of *all* contraceptive practices did not start with Pius XI. It is precisely in order to avoid this repeated condemnation of contraception that a few modern theologians (particularly Louis Janssens) have attempted to prove that, at least in the case of "the pill," no direct contraception is involved. This opinion will be discussed at the end of Chapter Four.

Meanwhile, the possibility still exists that the moral situation today has grown so complex that the principles on which the past rejection was based are no longer the only ones to determine a moral course of action. If this proved to be the case, the note of infallibility would certainly not apply to the condemnation of contraception in every circumstance, at least. In a recent article, Father Willem Van der Marck, O.P. seems to take this position, even though he restricts the discussion to the pill. Again, it will be necessary to postpone any final conclusion until after a more detailed consideration of the moral "situation" (Chapters Three and Four).

Finally, a word must be said about the opinion of certain authors who agree that the present Catholic position on artificial birth control is not infallible, and yet think it to be part of the deposit of faith.

---

tentione seminatio impeditur a naturali suo fine." Cajetan: *Commentarii in Summam Theologiae*, I-II, Qu. 154, Art. 1, No. XII.

Ford and Kelly quote the strange opinion of J. Fuchs, S.J. that the doctrine, although not infallibly proposed, is stated in such a solemn declaration "that one who is unwilling to admit it sins against the virtue of faith, although he does not lose the Faith."[5] And they themselves feel that it is "irrevocable" because it is "very likely already taught infallibly *ex jugi magisterio*": that is, if a survey were made of the teaching of the universal Church about contraception (as was done for the definition of the dogma of the Assumption), it might reveal that it is being infallibly proposed.[6] But the simple fact is that such an official survey was never made, and that if the two authors are sure of its outcome (as well as of the existence of an explicit and unanimous tradition), they cannot but consider it infallible by the ordinary teaching authority—which they are reluctant to do. So far as I can see there is nothing between infallible and fallible: whatever is not certainly infallible is not to be accepted as infallible today, even though it may very well be true and the object of an infallible definition in the future. But to say, on the one hand, that the present doctrine is not certainly infallible and, on the other hand, that "it must be included in some way within the object of infallibility" is to make a distinction so subtle that it escapes common logic. One has to draw the line somewhere.

However, the non-infallible character of the proposed doctrine by no means implies that it is not true, nor that the Church will eventually alter its basic stance. I myself am rather inclined to believe that this

5. Ford and Kelly, *op. cit.*, p. 269.
6. *Ibid.*, p. 270; 277.

will not happen—not because the position is irrevocable (for if it lacks the dogmatic note of infallibility, at least the possibility of error remains, and the only honest thing to do if one discovers that his position is no longer correct is to change it), but because the Church's *basic* teachings on the ends of marriage and of the marriage act are so obviously sound that only the utmost confusion in the justification of (and practical deductions from) these teachings could open them to honest doubt. What I rather expect is that the very complexity of the cases proposed to today's moral theologians, as well as their own growing awareness of the problems involved, will compel the experts to take a more sophisticated attitude both towards an articulation of the moral principles of the Church's basic teaching and towards their application.

CHAPTER 3

Natural End and Natural Law

Let us have a look now at the philosophical foundation of the present Catholic view on birth control. Here a serious discussion is most urgently needed. The situation has reached the point where teachers of moral theology openly admit that the "rational" arguments are not convincing and in the same breath claim that the Church's position is entirely based on reason. The way in which these arguments are presented sadly reflects the attitude of self-confident laziness which the outsider all too rightly detests in Catholic intellectuals when religion or morality are under discussion. We Catholics tend to take the ultimate truth of our Church so much for granted that quite often we do not bother to examine what this "truth" implies, even when the *magisterium* proposes it as rational and thereby urges us to probe its meaning with all possible industry.

A typical illustration of this self-defeating "fideism" is the incredible sloppiness with which the ordinary Catholic textbook in philosophy handles the rational foundations of Christian faith. The First Vatican Council defined that man, by the light of reason, is able to conclude to the existence of God. But what does the textbook philosopher do? Instead of following up the

hint and going to work on an argument that makes
sense to the man who lives after Hume, Kant, Hegel
and Marx, he simply rehashes a "proof" which was
fully completed before the "problem of God" in philosophy arose. Even that is usually stated only *pro
forma,* since the writer's own conclusion is reached by
an entirely different argument—and a very peculiar
one, indeed: The Vatican Council teaches that the
existence of God can be proven by the light of reason;
ergo, I can prove it, no matter how little use I make of
my reason. As to the philosophers who framed the
problematic within which the issue should be discussed, they are lucky to get away with a cursory dis-
missal in the "adversaries" paragraph. If the reader
happens to be unconvinced by these unconvincing
arguments, he is given some additional support by the
threat of not conforming to the infallible teaching of
the Church, and is thus ultimately invited to accept
the "rational arguments" in the name of faith. At the
end of this performance the pious writer pats himself
on the back for having put reason to the service of
faith. In fact, he has betrayed the serious task which
faith imposed upon him. Rather than following the
"sensus Ecclesiae," which he so presumptuously mo-
nopolizes, he has done the exact opposite of what was
expected from him. Instead of providing the rational
foundation for which the Council asked, he advocates
the abdication of the mind and insults the dignity of
man's intellect.

The same scandal will be created by the "rational
arguments" against birth control if we should fail to
submit them to a more careful scrutiny in the light of

the insight which we have today into human nature and the human condition. The least we can say is that, even if the present Catholic stand is based on sound principles, the rational articulation of these principles (which also has an impact on their application) must be reexamined.

The first thing which strikes one, and which makes a dialogue on this subject with non-Catholics very difficult, is that most arguments refer to the natural law, a principle which non-Catholics should be able to understand as well as Catholics. Yet, as it turns out, only Catholic Christians seem to have an insight into this point of the natural law. One sometimes wonders whether this emphasis on natural law is not simply due to the absence of any valid argument in Holy Scripture to support the Catholic position.

The most common argument based on natural law starts with the major premise that it is evil to separate an act which pursues a good of vital importance from its natural end. The minor premise states then that with the use of contraceptives the marriage act is always frustrated from its natural end. The conclusion follows that it therefore is always morally evil to use contraceptives and (because of the principle that in sexual matters "non datur parvitas materiae"—the matter is always serious), mortal sin is involved.[1]

1. This argument is proposed in different ways by various authors, but is always based on the intrinsic finality of the act of sexual intercourse. It will suffice here to quote one of the most respected textbooks in moral theology, Génicot-Salsmans's *Institutiones Theologiae Moralis*, Vol. II (Bruges, 1951), p. 460: "Malitia huius peccati in eo est quod completus usus venereorum seiungitur a fine suo naturali." "The moral evil of this

The first problem that arises is: What is the natural end of sexual intercourse? The answer that it is procreation is correct, but the implications of this finality are by no means as simple as the argument seems to assume. That *nature's* intrinsic purpose in sexual activity is procreation does not imply that every single act must necessarily lead to procreation, since nature itself does not attain this end in each individual act. It does so only in a small percentage of cases. The argument, therefore, should not be based on the actual effectiveness of the single act: "nature" has arranged things in such a way that a plurality of acts is required to make its intrinsic finality effective.

There is a difference between the intrinsic finality of nature as a whole and that of the individual act of intercourse; the latter, we recognize, does not attain its end in an absolute way, since nature itself has made ample provision for exceptions in the attainment of its end. The intrinsic finality of nature must be actualized if nature is to continue its existence, but this actualization is not bound to any individual act. This distinction between the absolute end of nature and the individual acts by which that end is achieved is both important and traditional. Without it we would be hard-pressed to assert that marital intercourse is morally licit in cases when the act will certainly not have its "natural" effect: during pregnancy, during menstru-

---

sin consists in the fact that a complete use of sexuality is severed from its natural end." Also Merkelbach, *Summa Theologiae Moralis*, 3 (Brussels, 1954), n. 955: "Onanism and any other kind of coitus that deprives the act of its natural relationship to generation is intrinsically against nature."

ation, after menopause, in the event of sterility. Moreover, although at one time it was, it is no longer considered immoral if—because of "serious motives such as those that are frequently included in what are called 'indications' (whether medical, eugenic, economic or social"[2])—married couples systematically and intentionally avoid conception by the rhythm method, although this is a deliberate attempt to have the act only under circumstances in which it cannot attain its natural end.

Here one might object that in rhythm at least the *course of nature* is respected, and consequently that in this case the individual intention is not incompatible with the intrinsic finality of the act. But the fact that nature is not effective in all its acts does not justify deliberate interfering in such a way that a particular act, which might have been effective, will now certainly be frustrated from its effect. The objection amounts to this, that one should not interfere with the course of nature in the attainment of its essential ends.

Now, if one understands by "nature" man's given biological apparatus, this is a strange way of reasoning indeed, for man constantly interferes with this nature in the most radical way, and no one ever thinks of calling this immoral.[3] No Roman Catholic today ob-

2. Pius XII, *Address to the Italian Catholic Union of Midwives* (Oct. 29, 1951).
3. "Frustration of nature far from being immoral is man's vocation. In the march of physical science and technology it means the progressively rational control of nature by man and for man. Man has always frustrated nature from the time he invented the first tool and will continue to do so until on his last day on earth he lays down his latest invention. And every canal

jects to vaccinations, injections of hormones, plastic surgery and amputation, when the good of *man* is at stake. Nor probably, will he object to medical intervention in order to induce regularity in a woman's cycle, an indication that in sexual life too, the Catholic is willing to accept interference.[4] Where, then, does the difference lie between all these interventions and artificial birth control?

That there is an essential difference between the artificial prevention of a physical evil, small-pox for example, and the interference with nature in the process of procreation is obvious enough: in the first case one helps or corrects physical nature to achieve its intrinsic end, in the other, one frustrates it from achieving this end; at least in a single, particular act. It is also clear that in a process as important as life itself, reasons

and every dam that man has built are monumental frustrations of nature's even flow. Fundamentalists, of course, will always greet each new tool with the cry 'Violation of nature' just as they did, for example, when drugs were introduced to lessen the pains of childbirth. When nature is deficient in doing what it should for human welfare, human art makes up for that deficiency. If this be frustration of nature the human cry is 'Give us more of it.' " Dr. Frederick Flynn, "Natural Law and the Overpopulation Problem," *The Catholic Messenger,* Davenport, Iowa, June 16, 1960.

The word "frustration" is unfortunate, since man's conscious intervention in all the cases which Dr. Flynn mentions is directed toward the perfection of nature's harmony, the realization of its immanent designs. Because of this confusion the quoted text is not immediately applicable to the present case. It must first be proved that birth regulation is more than a "frustration" of nature.

4. It should be remarked that, thus far, no absolutely reliable method for regulating the ovulatory cycle is available and that many physicians doubt whether it will be in the near future.

serious enough to justify interference with the course of nature in other domains would not be sufficient to justify interference in the process of procreation. It is a substantial leap, however, from these considerations to the assertion that, in the case of marital intercourse, the individual acts by which man's nature attains its vital ends are an *absolute*, unrelated to the totality of his spiritual life. Unfortunately, moralists in the past have been all too inclined to take this leap and to condone any kind of birth regulation as long as the material aspect of the sexual relations were "in order." Professor Janssens justly condemns this "terrible physicism, completely closed to true morality."[5]

In areas other than the sexual, moral theologians habitually avoid the dangerous abstraction of taking an act out of its human context. In explaining the Fifth Commandment, which is no less basic than the Sixth, they immediately grant that the preservation of life itself, the most basic end of man's nature, is not always an absolute value: moral theology has no qualms about killing in a just war or in self-defense, although the question of capital punishment is in a state of flux. It tells us that under certain circumstances a Christian has the right and even the obligation to lay down his life for higher values. Those who have done so are venerated as heroes and saints. Why, then, should this nature, or, more correctly, one particular act out the many by which it attains its purpose, become an absolute in marital intercourse?

Such a way of reasoning about nature contains, I feel, two basic flaws. It confuses man's biological struc-

5. Louis Janssens, *art. cit.*, p. 816.

ture with his human nature. And it takes human nature as a static, unchangeable thing, rather than as a principle of development.

Man's biological life and its intrinsic laws are but one aspect of human existence. To the extent that without them no other values can exist, life and the continuation of the human species are undoubtedly basic values. They are not absolute, however; and to absolutize one particular value, even the most basic, at the expense of all others is precisely what we call moral evil. The argument based on the equation of nature with man's biological structure and the way in which it attains its intrinsic end tends to make one value so absolute that it may compromise all others. A married couple, who for good physiological, economic or psychological reasons should have no more children, may find that for them rhythm is ineffective; if we force them to choose either abstinence from intercourse or the near certainty of more children, we impose on them an alternative in which values as essential as love and the well-being of their children are sacrificed. Such a decision would seem to require a more solid justification than reference to the intrinsic finality of man's biological nature.

Biological nature becomes sacred only when placed within the sacredness of *human* nature: no one objects to interfering with the biological functions of animals. Human nature is different from that of all other beings on earth precisely in that it is not entirely given once and for all; in man "nature" is never allowed to follow a course independent of "person." Man is not tied to his *given* physical nature as animals are; his instincts do not blindly execute the designs of his nature. He has instead a mind and a free will with which, within the totality of his spiritual existence, he must accept, develop, and even correct what is given to him. I do not eliminate the concept of a given nature, as if man by his freedom were able to create himself into anything he might want to be. Nor does man have the right to frustrate his *given nature* from the attainment of its basic ends. But I do assert that *human* nature is different from all other nature in that it is open, self-developing and, therefore, attains its ends in a way different from that of animals who merely follow the "course of nature."

To talk about human nature as if it were an immutable entity, given in its entirety, is to ignore the most essential characteristic of *human* nature. The same holds true for the natural law. People often seem to confuse the natural law with the unvarying and static laws of nature. They forget that man's natural law must necessarily be the law of a nature to whose essence growth and development belong. The natural law is certainly not a set of rigid and inflexible imperatives; it is the very law of man's ethical development. In this development there is an unchangeable element that forms the basis of the development itself: without this there would be no continuity and the very notion of a developing *nature* would be lost. But equally necessary is the development itself.

People seem to have no difficulty in accepting this on the practical level, but many bridle when it is stated theoretically. We all know that to kill another human being is against the natural law. Yet we see that there has been an enormous difference in the application of this general precept throughout the ages. For our Teutonic Christian ancestors capital punishment was left to the individual parties involved. Later, in a more organized society, what had been accepted as legitimate private punishment was rejected as a moral crime; today we wonder whether capital punishment, even when inflicted by public authority, is not against the natural law. The reason for this change in attitude is not, as one often hears, that the external circumstances have changed while man remains the same; on the contrary, the circumstances have changed mainly *because man has changed*. The natural law is the dynamic expression of this ethical development.

The Church itself has changed its position on important issues of the moral law in cases where there is no indisputable scripture evidence of a positive divine law to the contrary. The prohibition against lending money at interest is a familiar case in point. To say that the economic conditions have changed and that, therefore, only the application of the law has changed, is a poor explanation, for the concrete imperatives, the applications of the law, belong to the law itself, when this law is the law of an essentially developing nature.

Although usury is only an example, basically different from the case which we are discussing, it is definitely related to our argument. Both cases show a greater complexity of principles within the same situation than do, for example, suicide or fornication. Also, the problem of procreation is connected with some of the same economic and technological developments which are responsible for the change in attitude toward usury. In a precapitalist agricultural society lending at interest was not morally justifiable, whereas a high reproduction rate was not only an economic benefit but, because of underpopulation and infant mortality, a matter of survival and, therefore, an unqualified good.

Once again, I do not deny that there is an unchangeable element in the natural law, just as there is a stable element in human nature throughout all its development, but I do say, that if this unchangeable element is detached from the evolutionary aspect, it becomes abstract and meaningless as a concrete ethical norm. The general precept of justice remains true today as it was in a precapitalist society, and the principle of justice will never change. The same can be said about the basic precepts of the natural law regarding chastity and procreation in marriage. But these precepts have to be specified in their concrete applications, and the applications may change as man himself changes.

If the natural law is to provide a concrete norm for man's fundamental well-being, one can hardly maintain that the application of the general precept of procreation would be the same in a world where the population doubles in thirty-five years as in a world where it doubles in sixteen hundred years. Of course, population statistics cannot solve a moral problem, for even if they were to prove that over-population is an imminent danger for the essential well-being of mankind, the issue as to how the danger can morally be avoided remains undecided. Yet, demographic factors as well as psychological and economic factors are part of the total situation to which the general precepts of the natural law are to be applied. Only when applied to the concrete situation do these precepts become *practical* norms, for no moral principle can become practical before it confronts all other moral principles involved in a particular case. But it is obvious that man's present condition with respect to procreation is more complex than it ever was in the past, and that more principles are to be taken into account and balanced with each other.

This statement does not imply any sympathy for "situation ethics," according to which, because of the "uniqueness" of human existence, the applicability of general norms to individual cases is denied.[6] On the contrary, I firmly accept the normative character of universal precepts because human existence is universal as well as individual. But I believe that only after a careful scrutiny of the concrete situation can one decide *which* general precepts are involved. This position then, remains in conformity with the traditional principles of ethical theory.

St. Thomas himself makes a distinction in the natural law between general principles which are the same at all times and for all men, and the conclusions, the practical applications derived from these principles, which are true only *ut in pluribus*—in the majority of cases.[7] This distinction could never settle the dispute about contraception, since the whole question is whether artificial birth control goes against the first principles of the natural law or against a derived con-

6. On this point one may consult Karl Rahner: "On the Question of a Formal Existential Ethics," in *Theological Investigations,* Vol. II, Helicon Press, Baltimore, 1963, p. 217 ff.

7. *Summa Theologiae* I-II, q. 94, a.4.

clusion which could possibly allow for exceptions.[8] But it would seem that any concrete application of a general principle places it automatically among the "conclusions" in a situation where opposite principles meet. This by no means diminishes the obligatory character of the concrete moral precept; it merely takes it out of the irenic but abstract realm of universal ethical values and puts it in a situation where it is almost never alone in determining a line of action. Nor does it mean that every concrete ethical rule allows for exceptions, for certain precepts (as, for example, the one which for-

8. I am not sure that St. Thomas would consider every precept of the natural law which has to do with man's sexual life a primary precept rather than a secondary, as we tend to do. Discussing polygamy, he writes in his *Summa Theologiae* III, Supplement, q. 65: "Now, whatever renders an action improportionate to the end which nature intends to obtain by a certain work is said to be contrary to the natural law. But an action may be improportionate either to the principal or the secondary end, and in either case this happens in two ways. First, on account of something which wholly hinders the end. . . . Secondly, on account of something that renders the attainment of the principal or secondary end difficult, or less satisfactory, for instance, eating inordinately in respect of undue time. Accordingly, if an action be improportionate to the end, through altogether hindering the principal end directly, it is forbidden by the first precepts of the natural law, which hold the same place in practical matters as the general concepts of the mind in speculative matters. If, however, it be in any way improportionate to the secondary end, or again to the principal end, as rendering its attainment difficult, or less satisfactory, it is forbidden, not indeed by the first precepts of the natural law, but by the second, which are derived from the first, even as conclusions in speculative matters receive our assent, by virtue of self-known principles; and thus the act in question is said to be against the law of nature."

Applying this to the Patriarchs of the Old Testament, he continues in the next article: "As stated above, plurality of wives is said to be against the natural law, not as regards its first

bids adultery) will never enter into conflict with others. It does follow, however, that in the application of an ethical principle circumspection is demanded lest other principles become jeopardized.

It seems that the traditional arguments against contraception take the marital act out of its concrete situation, and then place this isolated, abstract act under an equally abstract moral precept. To be sure, the general precept of procreation remains valid and will always remain valid. But does it apply to every single act individually, regardless of the circumstances? Of course, no circumstances will ever make a good act out of a bad one. The whole question is, however: What makes the act good or bad? If the use of contraceptives is *destructive of an absolute value of man,* it is certainly evil, and no circumstances can ever change this fact. But whether it is destructive of such a value or not depends upon the circumstances in which the contraceptives are used. Father Francis Connell writes about the morality of actions of the bodily functions: "There is no act which is intrinsically wrong if it is considered *merely in itself,* without any modifying circumstances. In other words, when we say that an action is intrinsically evil from the moral standpoint,

---

precepts, but as regards the secondary precepts, which, like conclusions, are drawn from its first precepts. Since, however, human acts must needs vary according to the various conditions of persons, times, and other circumstances, the aforesaid conclusions do not proceed from the first precepts of the natural law, so as to be binding in all cases, but only in the majority; for such is the entire matter of Ethics, according to the Philosopher. Hence, when they cease to be binding it is lawful to disregard them."

we mean that the physical action *in a certain circum-stance or certain circumstances* is opposed to the nat-ural law of God and may never be allowed."[9] The use of contraceptives, then, becomes morally qualified by the situation in which the value of procreation may morally be obtained. For a woman in danger of being raped, to use contraceptives is morally good, since she is not in a situation in which procreation constitutes a morally pursuable value. When married couples choose to have intercourse, on the contrary, they are unques-tionably in the *objective* situation—and the only one —in which the continuation of human life is a basic value to be pursued.

Does this necessarily imply, however, that procrea-tion is always, for every married couple, under all circumstances, an absolute value? Can it still be called an absolute value when other values of equal or greater importance are being jeopardized, as, for example, the essential well-being of the living?

In *The Time Has Come*, Dr. John Rock raises the question of whether the protection which nature pro-vides for the fetus by supplying progesterone in order to exclude another ovum that would dangerously com-pete for maternal nourishment, could not be extended by deliberate intervention to the children already liv-ing.[10] Moralists might object that the two cases are not identical: for the living children competition from

9. *The American Ecclesiastical Review*, June 1964. The great moral authority of its author as well as the fact that he is firmly opposed to any form of contraception gives this statement all the more weight.

10. *The Time Has Come*, Alfred Knopf, New York, 1963, pp. 174-175.

another child is not a matter of life and death as it is for the fetus, and even if it were, there is always the possibility of continence. In this instance, nevertheless, Dr. Rock's argument seems to be basically sound, for the protection of life itself is not the only ground which justifies drastic measures. Moral theologians have always taught that force may be used against an unjust assailant (even if he is not formally guilty, because of insanity) to protect values considerably less important than life. On this basis one might conclude that the well-being of the living is a serious moral ground. We all know how this well-being can become seriously jeopardized by an undue extension of the family, or even, as psychiatrists have pointed out, by the complete continence of the parents.

CHAPTER 4

Recent Solutions and Their Theoretical Implications

If procreation were an *absolute* value in every single act of intercourse, then it could hardly be justified under circumstances where the act will certainly not lead to procreation. This line of thought can obviously not be pursued, for we know how the Church assents to the fact that intercourse is morally justified even though no procreation can follow and, what is more important, how during recent years she has approved of the emphasis on the secondary end of the act, the mutual fulfilment of the married people. It is no longer necessary to have the primary end as motive for every single act.

Even more interesting for this case are the solutions which have been given to marital problems over the last five years on the basis of principles which were never invoked before and which will probably lead to further conclusions. In an address to hematologists on September 12, 1958, Pope Pius XII made the following statement:

Is it licit to prevent ovulation by means of pills used as remedies for exaggerated reactions of the uterus and of the organism, although this medication, by preventing ovulation, also makes fecundation impossible? Is this permitted to the married woman who, despite this temporary sterility, desires to have relations with her husband? The answer depends on the person's intention. If the wife takes this medication, not with a view to preventing conception, but solely on the advice of a physician, as a necessary remedy by reason of a malady of the uterus or of the organism, she is causing an indirect sterilization, which remains permissible according to the general principle concerning actions having a double effect. But one causes a direct sterilization, and therefore an illicit one, whenever one stops ovulation in order to preserve the uterus and the organism from the consequences of a pregnancy which they are not able to stand. Certain moralists pretend that it is permitted to take drugs for this purpose, but this is a mistake. It is necessary likewise to reject the opinion of many physicians and moralists who permit the use of them whenever a medical indication renders a too early conception undesirable, or in other similar cases which it will not be possible to mention here; in these cases the employment of drugs has as its end the prevention of conception by preventing ovulation; there is question, therefore, of direct sterilization.[1]

The remarkable point here is that the Pope himself solves the case on the basis of the moral intention and not of the material act. Of course, as Fathers Ford and Kelly point out correctly, this is not to be understood as if the intention were the only criterion, for if the drug's sole effect were to suppress the procreative power, there would be direct sterilization involved and it would not be licit by this principle. But it has become increasingly difficult to draw a dividing line between direct and

1. *Acta Apostolicae Sedis*, 50 (1958), pp. 735-736.

indirect sterilization. Ford and Kelly are willing to allow a "rebound" therapy which consists in a temporary suppression of the ovulation in a sterile woman in order to increase the chances of fertility after that period. They conclude that suppression of ovulation, even when directly intended, is not necessarily the same thing as sterilization directly intended. The distinction becomes rather tenuous.

It becomes even more tenuous in the use of progestational compounds for psycho-therapeutic purposes, because here the fear of pregnancy would be a direct reason for using the drugs. This is what P. Anciaux, a leading Belgian theologian, has to say about the liceity of this practice, in a journal for the diocesan clergy of Malines, Belgium:

> We are of the opinion that this treatment can be justified if the psycho-medical indication is sufficiently serious, even though the distinction between "direct" and "indirect" sterilization here becomes extremely delicate. If a treatment with progestational compounds is really only one aspect of a psycho-therapeutic treatment, then, it seems to us, that physician and patient have to judge in conscience whether they consider it a justifiable treatment.[2]

A similar tendency is to be found in the opinion of several moralists[3] that steroids may be used during the

2. P. Anciaux: "Geboortenregeling en hormoonpreparaten." In: *Collectanea Mechliniensia* 30 (1960), p. 17. This text is quoted with approval in the *Collationes Brugenses et Gandavenses,* the journal for the clergy of Bruges and Ghent (1960), p. 134.

3. See L. Janssens in *Ephemerides Theologicae Lovanienses* 34 (1958), pp. 359-60.

period of lactation, even though the mother is not actually nursing her child. The solution is based on the fact (or belief?) that in the great majority of cases nature itself supposedly secures proper care for the newborn child by preventing further conception during the lactation period. Cases in which ovulation does take place could therefore be considered as pathological or at least as deviating from nature's normal "intentions" and, consequently, may be remedied by the use of steroids. Here we have an obvious case of direct sterilization which, however, is not illicit because it only prevents abnormal fertility. As one authority puts it: "The existence of a special hormonal mechanism that normally operates to inhibit ovulation during lactation is a sufficient indication of nature's intention."[4]

The problem of women with an irregular cycle is solved along the same lines. The use of steroids for three or four months would be morally acceptable if it should prove effective in regulating the cycle.[5] Regularity here is proposed as an ideal of nature itself, although irregularity, being so wide-spread, can hardly be called pathological. A positive determination of the 28-day cycle would therefore constitute a perfection of nature rather than a frustration. On that basis it is declared to be licit.

In all these cases one definitely gets the impression that the theologians are breaking away from the iso-

4. Denis O'Callaghan, "Correspondence," *Irish Theological Quarterly*, 28 (1961), p. 157.

5. The opinion was proposed by Francis J. Connell, C.SS.R. and John J. Lynch, S.J., and is supported by many theologians. See Ford and Kelly, *op. cit.*, pp. 352-360.

lated act (particularly in its purely material aspect) and more and more tend to see the act in its totality which includes both the intention and the effect. It is precisely for this reason that it has become increasingly difficult clearly to distinguish direct from indirect sterilization. Father W. Van der Marck, O.P. concludes:

> In the so-called "doubtful cases" where one can hardly speak of a serious medical indication, the moralists themselves have passed beyond the limits of the narrow situation of the act with double effect. They even came to acknowledge the existence of crises situations and self-defense, while at present there is a growing tendency to replace the term "sterilization" by "postponement of ovulation." It seems that we now have arrived at a point where moral science will be able to solve a problem which it has not yet formulated: how it is possible that "what in itself is anti-natural" and therefore *"per se* evil," the deprivation of marital intercourse from its natural power, which *nothing* can make "morally good" (Pius XI in *Casti Connubii*), can be made good, according to Pius XII. Indeed, he calls marital intercourse licit and good when hormone preparations are used for therapeutic purposes even though they are sterilizing. Much then must depend on "purpose" or "intention"—so much that any abstract statement about "what is in itself anti-natural" and *"per se* evil" can become completely meaningless in a concrete case.[6]

More and more the *finis operis* (the objective tendency of the act) is being seen in its unity with the *finis operantis* (the intention of the agent), as I think it should. To consider the *finis operis* alone leads to

6. William Van der Marck, O.P., "Vruchtbaarheidsregeling: poging tot antwoord op een nog open vraag," in *Tijdschrift voor Theologie*, 1963, p. 412.

biologism, but to isolate the *finis operantis* leads to subjectivism and, ultimately, to situation ethics. Human acts do have an objective meaning and finality which cannot be basically changed, and which ought to be respected. But this meaning is neither complete nor static: it is codetermined by the conscious intention through which the agent assumes it in the totality of his human existence. From this it follows: 1) that an act which would frustrate the intentions of nature altogether is self-contradictory and morally evil; 2) that nature is to be seen in its entirety (i.e. both biological and spiritual) as *human* nature.

I am not sure that all the conclusions have been drawn from this particular principle. Too many authors still speak about the intentions of nature without sufficiently emphasizing that this is the nature of a free and conscious being to whose essential dignity it belongs to correct and aid the biological apparatus whereever it is deficient in what could reasonably be expected for the well-being of the *totality* of human life. There still is a tendency to isolate the biological aspect of human nature. One often has the impression that moral theologians are more lenient to human intervention whenever it furthers the intentions of man's *biological* nature. In their discussion about the liceity of seminal tests and assisted insemination, Fathers Ford and Kelly write: "It might be suggested that theologians are more ready to approve seminal tests and assisted insemination because these procedures are for the promotion of fertility."[7] Why not extend this

7. Ford and Kelly, *op. cit.*, p. 365.

privilege to human nature as a *whole*? Why should the objectives of man's biological nature be more important than those of his total nature?

More and more theologians, however, seem to have become aware of the onesidedness of this view. Father O'Callaghan writes about the use of anovulants for the purpose of regularizing a woman's cycle:

> If this adjustment were made in order to ensure intercourse at the time of maximum fertility so that the chances of conception would be enhanced, one feels certain that no one would be found to condemn it. So too, when the purpose of this treatment is to make the use of the safe period more secure, the intention does not alter the moral judgement on the act. If married persons are entitled to restrict their intercourse to the safe period, they are entitled to make their use of it more effective by any lawful means which respects the natural context of reproduction.[8]

Father Lynch also refers to the *bonum totius* in his discussion of the same problem.

Yet, far from solving the problems, this total and progressive view of human nature still leaves us with the most difficult question: At which point exactly does the meaning-giving activity of the free agent conflict with the objective meaning of the act itself considered in its totality? Where does the interference with the functioning of nature become arbitrary—and, therefore, evil? Or, more concretely, to what extent could progesterone be used for its sterilizing effect if the most essential values of marital love and family

8. Denis O'Callaghan, "Fertility Control by Hormonal Medication," in *Irish Theological Quarterly*, 27 (1960), p. 13.

unity are at stake? Would this really be an arbitrary intervention in the functioning of man's biological nature?

Some moralists would object that in such a case, one would be pursuing the secondary end of marriage to the deliberate exclusion of the primary. But are the two ends of marriage so independent as to allow the dilemma that one cannot be abandoned without seriously harming basic human values and the other cannot be pursued without compromising equally essential values? I do not think that the two ends must be thus separated. Since the primary end of marriage is not simply procreation (as is the "natural" end of the *act* of marriage) but procreation *and* raising to adulthood of the offspring, it would seem that, at least in those cases where continence creates a tension between the parents which seriously harms the education of the children, the pursuit of the secondary end itself is essential for the *full* accomplishment of the primary end. Could one call, then, an intervention arbitrary, if it precludes further procreation only in order to fully accomplish the primary end?

As to the act itself, it is obvious that contraception prevents it from attaining its objective end, but only in part—for, as mentioned in Chapter One, the mutual fulfillment in love is an equally essential part of the total end. To be an expression of love belongs as much to the *intrinsic* and *objective* meaning of the marital act (and not merely to the subjective intention of the agent), as to be creative of new life. How much this is the case can be seen in Pius XII's condemnation of artificial insemination. If procreation were the only objective purpose of marital intercourse, why would a more efficient way of obtaining this purpose not be morally permissible? Yet, the Pope rejects it and thereby unmistakably implies that the interpersonal character of the marital act is part of its objective totality. Once one admits this, it becomes obvious that a possible conflict between love and procreation can no longer simply be dismissed as a resistance of an extrinsic intention (the *finis operantis*) to the one and only objective meaning (the *finis operis*) of the act.

But even if one excluded the subjective intention of the agent from the objective meaning of the act, a mere reference to the primary end of marriage would still not be a satisfactory argument against contraception. Authors who simply write that contraception is in conflict with the primary end of marriage (as, for example, Sabetti does in his *Compendium Theologiae Moralis*: "repugnant primario fini matrimonii"), seem to confuse the biological end of the marriage act, which is procreation, with the primary end of marriage itself, which is procreation and *raising to adulthood* of offspring. If the pursuit of the biological end of the marriage act comes into conflict with an essential part of the primary end of marriage itself, the question arises, which one is more important—the attainment of the biological end of the act, or the attainment of the full primary end of marriage. The alternative of complete continence (which is the only possibility in many cases) does not solve the difficulty if such continence harms the mutual love of the parents and thereby seriously affects the rearing of the children It would seem that in a conflict of the two, the act becomes subordinate to the more comprehensive finality of marriage itself. To consider marriage as a number of individual marital acts is to neglect the much more important aspect of the marital situation in its totality. This view seems to be confirmed by the fact that morally marriage can be had without the marriage act, whereas the act cannot be had without marriage.

Let it be made clear that I do not mean to imply that the secondary end of marriage becomes primary: both marriage and the marriage act are essentially directed towards procreation, and this end remains an absolute value for the human species. The act may therefore never be used in such a way that the attainment of this end, the continuation of the human species, would be frustrated or harmed. Nor may it be used, in any individual instance, for the attainment of the secondary end alone to the exclusion of part of the primary, when greater values do not interfere with the individual contribution to the attainment of this part of the primary end. Only when they do interfere, could the end of procreation in an individual instance become relative rather than absolute, and would the possibility exist that we might have to sacrifice it to a greater good. It is obvious, however, that mere pleasure could never justify the frustration of the marriage act from the attainment of its natural biological end.

So far we have not considered the question whether there is a moral difference between the use of anovulants when applied for their sterilizing effect, and mechanical contraceptives (e.g. a diaphragm). Most moralists would give a negative answer: whether the device is chemical or physical, the intended effect is the same. Yet, recently two theologians of the Low Countries, Professor Louis Janssens and Father Willem Van der Marck, O.P., have expressed a different opinion. Whereas "contraception" remains forbidden, the use of progesterone for the explicit purpose of excluding procreation could be declared licit under certain circumstances. Professor Janssens justifies this use of steroids on the ground of its similarity to the rhythm method which is morally permissible even though it deliberately excludes the possibility of procreation. Progesterone respects the mechanism of procreation at least as much as the rhythm method does.

> While periodic continence speculates, in the course of each cycle, on the disintegration of the ovum to prevent it from using its reproductive power, progesterone preserves the ova and their reproductive function for the time when the married couple judge that their duty of generous fecundity calls for procreative acts.[9]

Progesterone, therefore, should not be called a contraceptive: it does not interfere with the reproductive mechanism, but only with its timing.

Someone might object that the *timing* is part of the total moral object and that, therefore, a deliberate intervention in the timing of the procreative mechanism has a moral impact upon all subsequent acts of intercourse which were intended with it. Professor Janssens would admit this but, as he points out, a deliberate timing of the procreative power does not *necessarily* pervert the morality of the procreative act.

9. Louis Janssens, "Morale conjugale et progestogènes," *Ephemerides Theologicae Lovanienses,* 1963, p. 822.

Indeed, the practice of rhythm is morally licit, even though it uses the time element *in order to* exclude conception. True enough, the rhythm method does not interfere with the physical course of nature. Yet the time element is an essential part of the intention, and thereby undoubtedly enters into the total *moral object* which includes, besides the physical act, the intention and the essential circumstances. What happens in the practice of rhythm? Procreation is certainly excluded from the intention. But it is also excluded by the choice of the means: the object of the choice is not just any conjugal act, but an act posited precisely and deliberately at a moment expressly chosen because it occurs in a sterile period.[10]

Yet, there remains one point in Professor Janssens' argument which requires further clarification. Why exactly is a deliberate interference with the timing *morally* different from the interference with the mechanism of procreation itself which takes place in the use of contraceptives? If the intended time is part of the moral totality of the act, as Professor Janssens admits, one might still ask why a *positive* intervention to regulate the timing of the procreation would morally differ from a positive interference with the mechanism itself. Also, I would be very hesitant to use the *physical integrity* of the marital act as an argument in favor of the pill, for any such consideration tends to isolate the physical aspect of the act from its moral totality, and will easily degenerate into the sort of abstract "physicism" from which Professor Janssens is trying to escape. Finally, undue emphasis on the fact that the pill does not interfere with the marital act itself, will undoubt-

10. *Ibid.*, p. 817.

edly provoke the reply of many moralists that the distinction between any sort of positive intervention *before* and *during* the act of intercourse is morally negligible, as long as this intervention directly influences the effect of the act.

In raising this difficulty, I by no means suggest that a positive intervention would *per se* be morally wrong. Nor is it implied that the distinction between pill and contraceptives *is* morally irrelevant. The physiological and psychological differences between the two are so important that they may very well result in an essential moral distinction. I merely say that the last word on this subject has not been spoken—no more, for that matter, than on the liceity of the pill.

In the meantime, Professor Janssens has made an important contribution to the discussion by placing the marital act in its total moral context of intention, effect and circumstances. He has done this by showing that this act has two meanings—procreation, and the expression of love—both of which must be considered in deciding what is morally permissible. I would like to add that, for a moral evaluation, the act itself must be seen in the light of the larger end of *marriage*, of which it is a partial realization. The important point, then, is not so much whether the physical integrity of the act, or of the biological mechanism, is preserved, but whether the act is in line with the essential finality of *marriage itself*. Here one must remember that this finality is twofold: 1) procreation and raising to adulthood of the offspring, 2) mutual fulfilment of the marriage partners. As we have seen in the previous chapter, the fulfilment of the secondary end is essential for the *complete* fulfilment of the primary end insofar as it includes the education of the children: where the love of the parents becomes jeopardized, the education of the children suffers. The question of the physical integrity of the procreative mechanism remains subordinate to the more important one: whether the act is in conformity with the end of marriage. Only in this wider perspective can one unblock some of the problems that are insoluble in a discussion restricted to a consideration of the isolated act.

Another defender of the pill, Father Willem Van der Marck, takes his starting point from the evolution which has occurred in moral theology on the transplantation problem. Until ten years ago, transplantation of human organs was judged exclusively in terms of mutilation and, since mutilation is permissible only for the good of one's *own* organism, declared illicit. Yet, gradually a new view developed which grasped the various physical phases of the transplantation process in their intentional totality. Transplantation was no longer seen as an act of mutilation, performed in order to make possible a second act of service to one's fellow man. The one good intention unites the successive stages of the process into one moral act.

It is characteristic of the human act that the physically distinguished elements can be united by the one meaning-giving purpose. The intention determines what the human act is, not only with respect to its "purpose," but also with respect to "the means." This implies that in the present case the first intervention, precisely as human act, is already transplanation. For to the extent that this intervention is "means," it is determined, as human act, by the end. Consequently, there is no question of mutilation, at least not of intended or "direct" mutilation. In other words, there is no mutilating action used as a means to aid one's fellow man. There is only transplantation.[11]

A similar judgment could be made on the use of progesterone for the purpose of birth regulation. In itself birth regulation is a moral good. Yet, theologians reject the pill as immoral, because it attains this good end *by means of* a previous act of sterilization—which is evil. Father Van der Marck disagrees with this opinion: the moral evaluation of the intervening act depends upon the moral character of the final end toward which the act is directed, and in the case of birth regulation, this end can be good.

Of course, as he points out, the final end could never save the morality of the total act if the use of anovulants were *evil in itself*, for then it would simply justify an immoral means by a good intention. However, the physical act of using progesterone remains *morally indifferent* until its moral character is determined by the end for which it is to be used. Theologians agree that the use of hormonal compounds for therapeutic purposes is licit. Now, since birth regulation is as much a good as the well-being of the body, there is no reason why anovulants could not be taken for this purpose.

Father Van der Marck objects to the traditional way of posing the problem which reduces all non-therapeutic use of the pill to an act of direct sterilization. To take the pill for the purpose of birth regulation (wher-

11. Willem Van der Marck, O.P., "Vruhtbaarheidsregeling: poging tot antwoord op een nog open vraag," in *Tijdschrift voor Theologie*, 1963, p. 401.

ever it is a moral good) is not to posit *first* an illicit act
of sterilization and *then* to achieve a good end. The
overall intention covers the entire process. If the end
is good, the various indifferent acts which lead up to
it will be good; if the end is bad (for example, through
a lack of generosity in achieving the primary end of
marriage), the entire process will be evil. The ultimate
moral judgment on the pill, then, is the same as that
on the rhythm method: the final answer depends on the
intention for which the method is used.

Much as I agree with Father Van der Marck's way
of posing the problem, it would seem that some of his
implicit assumptions are open to question. He defends
the pill for the purpose of birth regulation, while rejecting "contraception" as intrinsically evil. Instead
of the traditional disjunction, "the use (of hormonal
compounds) is either therapeutic or sterilizing, that is,
contraceptive,"[12] he offers a third possibility: the use
of anovulants for the purpose of a morally licit birth
regulation.

But what is this "contraception" which is rejected
from the outset? The author avoids defining it. In the
light of his article I do not see how he could describe
it in any way other than *either* as the use of any means
to prevent conception for a purpose that is not morally
good, *or* as the use of *mechanical* (as opposed to chemical) means to prevent conception. The second alternative conflicts with his entire theory, since the import
of this theory is precisely that the various physical
stages are united in the total intention which determines the one human act. The distinction, then, be-

12. *Art. cit.*, p. 399 (my italics).

tween an intervention *before* and *during* the act of intercourse is no longer morally relevant. Nor can one say that the use of chemical devices is morally indifferent while that of physical contraceptives is not, for the distinction between physics and chemistry is equally irrelevant from a moral viewpoint.

Consequently, to remain consistent with his own theory, Father Van der Marck must take the first alternative: contraception is the use of *any* means which prevent conception, *for a purpose which is not morally good.* But then it is not easy to see why the author can say that *only* anovulants are permissible for a morally good purpose. What difference can there be between the pill and, for example, a diaphragm, if both are used with the same intention? The fact that anovulants, unlike mechanical devices, *can also* be used for therapeutic purposes does not affect the moral evaluation of their use for the clear purpose of birth regulation. The reasons, then, why Father Van der Marck advocates the pill while rejecting "contraceptives" must be entirely extrinsic to his argument. I can think of no other reason than that mechanical means have been rejected, without qualification, in the encyclical *Casti Connubii,* while the current rejection of anovulants is restricted to their use for the purpose of direct sterilization. Yet, this reason is somewhat surprising for an author who so generously allows for evolution in papal pronouncements.[13]

Father Van der Marck's preference for the pill as opposed to "contraceptives" on the ground that the pill does not interfere with the marital *act itself* (as

13. See, for instance, the text quoted on Page 57 of this book.

he explicitly notes in the English summary of his article), is not very consistent with his own argument, and returns to the very division of the human act which he rejects in his article.

This criticism by no means implies that there might not be an essential distinction between pill and "contraceptives." It merely confirms what I said in my comments on Janssens: the distinction has not been sufficiently clarified.

The present position of the problem could be summarized in this statement of the Dutch hierarchy:

> Even though the oral, chemical means which are now propagated for preventing conception cannot be accepted as a *generally applicable solution,* any more than the instrumental means which have been known for a long time, Catholic morality discusses the question whether the use of these means could be accepted in certain situations.[14]

All this leaves the Catholic Christian with a practical problem. Which opinion is he to follow as long as the magisterium has not made a final decision on the issue? In the diocesan newspaper of Steubenville, Ohio, Father Francoeur estimates the opinion of those theologians who have spoken out in favor of the pill as "certainly and solidly probable." This would imply that, according to the most prevalent moral system in the Catholic Church today, Probabilism, a Catholic may follow the opinion of the advocates of the pill, even if he considers it less probable than that of those who declare its use illicit. It is by now generally known

14. The words in italics have, strangely, been dropped in two English translations.

that Father Francoeur's view could be supported by the privately expressed opinions of some of today's leading theologians, although these have never been expressed in writing as yet.[15] On the other hand, on June 23, 1964 Pope Paul VI asserted that the opinions of Pius XII were to be followed until such time as a more detailed statement on the question—now in preparation—could be concluded.

But these practical solutions do not settle the theoretical problem. The fact that an uncertain law does not bind in conscience by no means implies that there is no law. Nor does the Pope's statement imply that the Catholic, and particularly the theologian, may cease his quest for certainty. The very fact that even the basic principles are not sufficiently clear to guide the individual conscience should urge the moralist all the more to find a satisfactory answer.

15. The special issue of *Commonweal* (June 5, 1964) on responsible parenthood (which came too late to be used for this book) contains, among several interesting pieces, an article by Father Haering. In it he locates the particular issue of "birth control" within its proper context of responsible growing love and the moral "law of growth." This issue also contains the relevant part of an interview with Eduard Schillebeeckx, O.P., which first appeared in *De Linie*.

CHAPTER 5

Psychological Arguments

As the natural law argument lost more and more of its appeal, a new approach was tried to solve the problem of artificial birth control. Arguments of a more empirical nature were sought to demonstrate that contraception is psychologically harmful and therefore (this seems to be the tacit implication) morally illicit. Unfortunately, most arguments fail to prove the first part as well as the second when they are applied to a real crisis situation. This is not to say that they are completely invalid.

One cannot but agree with Father de Lestapis' well-founded criticism of a "contraceptive civilization," and with his rejection of a decadent hedonism which probably constitutes a greater threat to our civilization than the population explosion.[1] Yet, our problem is not: Has the universal use of birth control for any purpose an unfavorable impact on society and individual? It is: Is the argument by which this thesis is proven also

1. Stanislas de Lestapis, S.J., *Family Planning and Modern Problems*, Herder and Herder, New York, 1961. It would be unfair to reduce this distinguished theological, psychological and demographic study to a mere argument against artificial birth control. Yet, the purpose of this book requires me to look at it from that angle only.

applicable to a crisis situation where the motive is not uncontrolled search for pleasure, but a matter of the preservation of the essential well-being of parents and children? I find no sufficient evidence in Father de Lestapis' book to answer the latter question affirmatively. However, I am not at all sure that the author intended to answer this question.

Let us, therefore, take an argument which certainly intends to show the immorality of artificial birth control under any circumstances. In their textbook on moral theology, Fathers John A. McHugh and Charles J. Callan write:

> The happiness and success of the home depend chiefly on the respect which its members have one for the other and on the cultivation of the sturdy virtues that strengthen character. The husband and wife who practise onanism and other similar carnal vices cannot have the mutual respect they should have; the wife is deprived of the treasure of her modesty and is treated as a prostitute rather than as an honored wife and mother, and the husband is brutalized by the removal of the natural restraint to his sex passion—such self-indulgent persons would either selfishly neglect the one or two children they may have or will spoil them for life by the luxury and laziness in which they are reared.[2]

We can ignore the implication that the majority of non-Catholic married women in civilized countries today are being treated as prostitutes and the false assumption that the real problem under discussion involves families with one or two children rather than those with five or more. I do seriously and strongly object to this argument based on happiness. It is an

2. *Moral Theology,* II (New York: 1958), p. 615.

empirical argument and can easily be rebutted. For people with real problems, the procreation of children beyond their psychological, physiological or economic possibilities leads in most cases to unhappiness both for the parents and for the children, and so does the alternative of complete continence. Still, I do not see how unhappiness alone could be a sufficient reason to practice contraception, any more than happiness alone would be a decisive argument against it.

It is precisely for this reason that psychological arguments for or against birth control are seldom decisive. Freud in his early days was in favor of contraception; in his later days he wrote against it.[3] Neither position is decisive in judging moral issues. The psychologist works on an empirical, descriptive level. His conclusions, therefore, can never settle a moral, normative problem. What he can do is clarify the concrete human situation in which the moral norms are to be applied.

In showing that a certain behavior is psychologically harmful, he renders an indispensable service to the moralist who now knows the real situation and judges which moral principles are to be applied in order to preserve man's essential values. But most of the time the psychologist is unable to do this in such a way that his conclusions apply to all individuals, even at one time and for one particular civilization. There is no doubt that contraception, particularly certain forms of it, may cause a frustration both in the expression of love and in sexual satisfaction that is worse than the hardships resulting from too many children or complete

3. Sigmund Freud, *A General Introduction to Psychoanalysis,* tr. Joan Riviere, Garden City, 1935, p. 277.

continence. Yet, this is not generally true, particularly not when oral contraceptives are used.

But even if psychological evidence were conclusive one way or another, the moralist would still have to decide to what extent man's psychological well-being may determine a moral issue. More important values than the individual's psychological well-being may be at stake. It is obvious that no psychological reason, no matter how serious, could ever be an objective justification for killing a person. For the same reason I would deem a purely psychological argument insufficient to make contraception permissible. But, likewise, it is also necessary to reject psychological arguments against birth control as inconclusive. A moral problem can be solved only by a science which encompasses *all* human values and is able to place them in the right hiearchy. Psychology is certainly not in a position to do this; it can clarify a moral situation but it cannot prescribe a line of action.

Yet, a new psychological argument has been used lately which, rather than considering individual happiness, concentrates on the objective meaning of the human act within the totality of human existence. This phenomenological approach is no longer purely empirical, as the psychological argument usually is: it analyzes the objective structure of the act itself and not the subjective experience of the agent. The argument is all the more compelling in that it never isolates the physical act but places it in a personalistic context. Father Paul Quay's excellent treatment, *Contraception and Marital Love,* offers an interesting example of this approach. With several other authors on marital love

(Gabriel Marcel, S. de Lestapis, S.J.), he considers the act of marriage as a symbol of self-donation. Since the act symbolizes the gift of the entire person, any basic reservation in the surrender contradicts the meaning of the act itself and, since it is so fundamental to man's entire existence, must in one form or another constitute moral evil. Now, Father Quay argues, this is precisely what happens in the use of contraceptives.

> The woman who uses a diaphragm seals off physically the most intimate part of her body and thus, in symbol, closes the depths of her spirit to her husband. She has accepted his affection but not his substance. . . . Love that is profound, however, does not deliberately frustrate its most nearly adequate mode of expression. . . . That first contraceptive act declares that much as one loves the other, one does not love enough to forego the pleasure of intercourse so that he or she might reserve for the other the most fitting expression of their love.[4]

Let us remark first that the argument deals exclusively with physical contraceptives rather than with sterilizing drugs which do not seal off any part of the woman's body. Yet, this objection does not invalidate the argument, for the meaning of the act of love lies in a surrender *tending towards creation*: a systematic exclusion of this creative aspect, therefore, runs counter to the act's objective and total significance. My problem with the argument is more basic. It would seem to me that the meaning of the act of marriage is determined not only by the totality of man's spiritual life, but also by the fact that he has to express his love in a repetition of acts over a period of time. Man is

4. Paul M. Quay, S.J., *Contraception and Marital Love,* Washington, D.C., 1961, pp. 18-20.

unable to express himself once and forever—he lives his existence in time.

In discussing the rhythm method, we have already learned that the time element enters into the intention of the act. But this principle holds true for any act of marital intercourse. The fact that every single act is essentially one of a series prevents it from being a "total" expression—as a unique act would be. To deprive the act permanently or constantly of its tendency toward procreation, would definitely imply a basic reservation in the surrender and thus contradict the objective meaning of the marital act. This is so much the case that the Church declares invalid a marriage contract in which man and woman *deny* each other the *right* to relations which might lead to procreation.[5] But for two marriage partners who have repeatedly proven their intention of complete surrender in creative acts of love, to exclude occasionally the fertility of their love when circumstances prevent them from taking proper care of new offspring, does not necessarily contradict the objective meaning of the marital act.

It would seem to me that the full meaning of these occasional acts can be grasped only by connecting them with the totality of all others, just as the meaning of the individual act of love can be understood only when it is placed in the totality of man's existence as a person. Unless we view the expression of love in its continuation in time, even the use of rhythm would be irreconcilable with the full meaning of the marriage act.

5. This is not the same as a mutual agreement to use contraceptives.

But there is another point in the phenomenological argument which has to be qualified. Father Quay considers the physical act of intercourse a *symbol* of surrender, and rightly so. Yet, this spiritual significance does not necessarily imply that the material act is simply to be accepted from nature, and that if it is at all modified it must lose its meaning altogether. Even an objective symbol is never completely given and preformed. Man receives his symbols from nature, but at the same time he *lives* them and, in living them, transforms them. A symbol which is not concretely lived is no longer a symbol; it becomes an empty shell. There seems to be, then, a certain freedom left, even in the most natural symbol, for the way in which man actually lives and interprets it, and without this freedom the symbol loses its symbolic meaning altogether.

What I am saying here is basically the same as what I wrote earlier about the relation between the *finis operis* and the *finis operantis*. The act itself has an objective meaning of its own, but this meaning is not finished—it is to be completed by the intention of the agent. That is why I do not believe that a phenomenological analysis alone of the marriage act and its meaning could ever settle the moral issue. The freedom of man's interpretation of natural symbols would seem to make such an analysis insufficient to provide him with the norms needed for moral action.

CHAPTER 6

Conclusion

In these considerations I have mainly tried to get the discussion on birth control away from an abstract level where it does not belong, and to replace the act of marital intercourse in its concrete human context. The main theses were: 1) To build an argument against contraception on the sacredness of nature (understood in such a way that the "natural" course of the marriage act excludes any deliberate interference) is to withdraw this act from the sphere of the properly human, even for the attainment of its natural, biological end. Such a position is obviously untenable. If, by some impossible hypothesis, periodic contraception were necessary to assure the continuation of the human species, it would at once become not only permissible but obligatory. 2) An argument built on the biological end of the act alone is equally unsatisfactory, for this biological end is only one facet of the total end of *man* toward which the act, as any human act, is directed, and which encompasses the essential well-being of the human person (materially and spiritually) both as individual and as species-being. This total finality is not extrinsic to the act; it is essential to its meaning as a *human* act, and it is the very element which makes the act sacred.

I have deliberately avoided going into the problem of the population explosion, first of all because I am not competent in this matter, but also because a sociological analysis by itself cannot decide a moral issue: it can only clarify the situation to which moral principles are to be applied. In the meantime, we have to admit that there is a very real problem which will eventually threaten the well-being of the entire human race.[1] How we cope with it is a moral question which must be answered in terms of human acts in relation to their total effects. If the world, or one particular part of it, is overpopulated, then this fact should be considered as part of the total effect of the act and must enter into our moral considerations.

It is noteworthy that ancient theologians, in dealing with the moral problems of onanism and fornication, solved them, not in terms of the isolated act, but in terms of the good of mankind (the population of the world which, until very recently, was an unqualified good). In the *Summa Contra Gentiles*, St. Thomas draws the discussion on fornication away from the loss of semen and the conservation of the individual, and places it in the perspective of the propagation of the

1. As such the problem must be studied, and Catholics have no right to decline their responsibility in these matters. Georgetown University recently started a *Center for Population Research*. This is a major step in the right direction.

species. This argument when applied to birth control seems to be much more solid. Yet its validity depends on the fact that propagation of the species is an unqualified good, which it certainly was in an agrarian society chronically suffering from underpopulation. Is it still valid everywhere today? And, what is of greater urgency, will it still be valid tomorrow? I prefer to leave the answer to sociologists and economists. But even if overpopulation were a fictitious problem, we still have the hard pressing problem today in Catholic homes, where the initial desire to realize the Christian ideal of marriage so often results in bitterness and estrangement from Christianity altogether.

Unfortunately, the whole issue has become obfuscated by the fact that too many people forget that authentic *human* love cannot be attained without self-control.[2] Nothing could be further from the intention of this book than to derogate from this fundamental principle. To establish the physical expression of love as an *absolute* value within marriage is to lapse into the very error I have been opposing here; it is to take the act of love entirely out of its total spiritual context. I have argued against absolutizing the value of procreation. But the same argument applies to the physical expression of love.

The marriage act is undoubtedly of great value, and in some cases it may be essential to the survival of marital love. But to consider it as an absolute value to be pursued even at the expense of all others is to

2. See Cardinal Suenens' beautiful book, *Love and Control,* Newman, Westminster, 1961.

isolate it from the totality of existence. Such a view would conflict more with the total finality of man than the one criticized in this book. Indeed, from the position advanced here it follows that *ideally*, that is, whenever the essence of marriage is not jeopardized, continence (either periodic or prolonged) remains *the* solution for a married couple unable to provide for more children, since in continence alone no major value is being sacrificed—always supposing that neither marital love nor the education of the children suffer from it. Our psychologizing generation is all too easily inclined to consider the tension which may result from continence as the supreme evil in life, and to forget that it might lead to a deepening of affection. Contemporary French writers on marriage claim that continence can have a most invigorating effect on love.

On the other hand, it seems to be a demonstrable fact that not every couple is able to attain the highest level of spiritual love, certainly not at once. In man's moral and spiritual life, no less than in his physical life, we must allow for growth and development. As Msgr. Bekkers, Bishop of s'Hertogenbosch (Holland) recently said in a television speech:

The Church knows that what one person can reach cannot always be reached by others. And then the Church wants to give room for a gradual, perhaps slow and imperfect growing such as is possible in all other areas of life; for instance, in charity, honesty and piety. The Church holds that those who keep on trying, although they have not reached the highest level, are on the right path.

It is conceivable that many people will never have the spiritual and psychic stamina to live up to this ideal. But the ideal remains.

It would be ill-advised to interpret this dynamic view as a reduction of moral precepts to mere counsels. The moral precepts are obligatory for everyone: no circumstances can dispense a normal human being from the basic generosity required to observe them. But there is another element in the moral law which goes beyond the precepts and which, in the case of marriage, calls for a gradual spiritualization of one's love. Now, if continence is always a *precept* in cases where fertility is undersirable, then the matter is settled and further discussion is useless; but if in certain cases it is rather an *ideal*, because the value in question cannot be obtained without, at least momentarily, compromising more important values, then other considerations must be taken into account. Indeed, if two married people are unable to live in prolonged continence without extreme tension, which deteriorates their own relationship and thus jeopardizes the well-being of their children, the question arises whether in attempting to live by a code of moral heroism for which they are not prepared, they are not sacrificing an *essential* perfection, to an *accidental*.

Again, I do not *deny* that the pursuit of procreation is an essential perfection, under any circumstances, for every married couple that has marital relations, but I question it because of the fallacies in the arguments by which this thesis is defended. I readily admit that *ideally* the highest perfection would consist in having the marriage act with all its consequences, or in not having it at all when those consequences cannot be accepted. But I wonder whether this ideal is always an essential perfection which man cannot omit without violating the moral law. If it is not, then we can only conclude that *le mieux est parfois l'ennemi du bien,* and that a person should not be called immoral because he has not reached the heights of perfection.

Christianity is a difficult religion, but it is not simplistic. It has probably set up a higher moral code than any ethical system in all the ages. But at the same time, it has always taken a starkly realistic view of human nature and its limitations. It was founded on the Cross, and cannot be practiced outside the law of the Cross. But it is also a religion based on the Resurrection; it is solicitous of life and love.

The questions raised here must be answered in the light of these principles. For a Catholic, arguments alone are insufficient in matters where the Church has chosen to lead the faithful; the final answer must come from the Church. But I think that this answer has not yet been given, and that ultimately it might vary somewhat from what moral theologians teach publicly today[3]: not because of a basic change in stance, but because of increasing insight into the complexities of the problem.

3. In their personal convictions, many moralists are far more advanced than in their publications. It is regrettable that at least the technical publications do not reflect more of the doubts concerning the traditional position which are so widespread in theological circles.

Even if this should be the case, however, it will not make things easier for the Christian. Instead of living by a universal and well-defined precept, he would have to return to his own conscience and decide, in his full responsibility before God, how he must respond to his vocation to create in Christ.

Bibliography

The following list is not intended as a complete bibliography on the moral problem of birth control. It includes only recent publications, particularly in English, which shed some new light on the subject. The listing by no means implies that the authors agree with the views defended in this book—simply that they are of particular interest for the position here outlined. In most instances a brief summary of the main line of argument has been added for the convenience of the reader.

P. Anciaux. "Geboortenregeling en hormoonpreparaten." *Collectanea Mechliniensia,* 30 (1960), p. 17.

> Sterilizing drugs may be used for psychotherapeutic purposes.

Mgr. W. Bekkers. (Television speech). *Herder Correspondence,* Vol. 0, No. 0, October 1963, p. 28.

In birth control, as in many other matters, we must allow for a growth in generosity. Not everyone is able to achieve the ideal of complete continence.

Francis J. Connell, C.SS.R. "The Morality of Ovulation Rebound." *American Ecclesiastical Review*, 143 (Sept. 1960), pp. 203-205.

Discusses the liceity of a temporary suppression of ovulation in a sterile woman to increase the chances of fertility subsequently.

————. "Is Contraception Intrinsically Wrong?" *American Ecclesiastical Review*, (June 1964).

The morality of an act dealing with bodily functions always depends on the circumstances—such an act is never evil if taken merely in itself.

A. M. Dubarle, O.P. "La Bible et les Pères ont-ils parlé de la contraception?" *Supplément de la vie spirituelle* (1962), pp. 573-610.

Authoritative discussion of the Scripture and early Fathers on contraception: it was never clearly rejected before St. Augustine.

Dutch hierarchy. *Letter to the Clergy. America*, April 18, 1964, p. 531.

The present stand of the Church on the problem of oral contraceptives, as seen by the Dutch hierarchy. (The translation in *America* misses an important qualification which the reader can find on p. 70 of this book.)

John C. Ford, S.J. and Gerald Kelly, S.J. *Contemporary Moral Theology II—Marriage Questions*. Newman Press, 1963, pp. 263-271.

The best study in moral theology on marital questions available in the English language. Particularly good is the discussion of the "cases."

Frederick Flynn, "Natural Law and the Overpopulation Problem," *The Catholic Messenger*, Davenport, Iowa, June 16, 1960.

The first article in the United States that called attention to the ambiguities in the notion of natural law as it is used in discussions on birth control.

Robert T. Francoeur. Letter. *The Steubenville Register*, Vol. XIX, No. 8, April 16, 1964, pp. 1, 5.

The arguments in favor of "the pill" may be considered solidly probable and can therefore be followed even by priests who are not personally convinced by them.

William J. Gibbons, S.J., and Thomas K. Burch, "Physiologic Control of Fertility: Process and Morality." *The American Ecclesiastical Review*, 138 (April, 1958), pp. 246-277.

An early examination of possible physiological means of regulating fertility, together with a moral evaluation in the light of moral theology and papal pronouncements.

Louis Janssens. *Ephemerides Theologicae Lovanienses*, 34 (1958), pp. 359-60.

Steroids may be used during the period of lactation to prevent a conception which in normal cases does not occur during this period.

———. "Morale Conjugale et Progestogènes," *Epheme-*

rides Theologicae Lovanienses, Dec. 1963, pp. 787-826.

> Defends the liceity of the pill even when used for the sole purpose of birth regulation.

Joseph E. Kerns, S.J. *The Theology of Marriage: The Historical Development of Christian Attitudes towards Sex and Sanctity in Marriage.* Sheed and Ward, New York, 1964.

> A survey of the attitudes in the Church—from the early Fathers to today—towards marriage and marital love.

Stanislas de Lestapis, S.J. *Family Planning and Modern Problems.* Herder and Herder, New York, 1961.

> An autoritative study of the demographic aspects of the problem of birth control and its moral implications.

John J. Lynch, S.J. "Moral Aspects of Pharmaceutical Fertility Control." *Proceedings of the Thirteenth Annual Convention of the Catholic Theological Society of America* (1958), pp. 127-38.

> A review of the question of pharmaceutical fertility control, distinguishing various types of drugs as to *finis operis.*

———. "Notes on Moral Theology." *Theological Studies,* 23 (June, 1962), pp. 233-65.

Denis O'Callaghan. "Fertility Control by Hormonal Medication." *Irish Theological Quarterly,* 27 (1960), p. 13.

Anovulants may be used for the purpose of regularizing a woman's cycle.

————. "Correspondence." *Irish Theological Quarterly,* 28 (1961), p. 157.

A response to objections against his contention that the use of anovulatory preparations to assist nature in suppressing ovulation during the lactation period does not involve direct sterilization and hence may be licit.

Pius XII. "Address to the Italian Catholic Union of Midwives." *Acta Apostolicae Sedis,* 43 (1951), pp. 835-854.

On the liceity of the rhythm method.

————. "Address to Hematologists." *Acta Apostolicae Sedis,* 50 (1958), pp. 732-40.

Indirect sterilization is morally permissible for therapeutic purposes.

Paul M. Quay, S.J. *Contraception and Marital Love.* Washington, D.C. 1961.

Psychological and phenomenological arguments against contraception.

Responsible Parenthood. A Special Issue. *The Commonweal,* June 5, 1964.

This issue contains eight articles which succinctly articulate the present state of the question.

John Rock. *The Time Has Come.* Knopf, New York, 1963.

Authoritative exposition on the medical and psychological aspects of "the pill."

Cardinal Leo Suenens. *Love and Control.* Newman, Westminster, Md., 1961.

A general treatment directed to those engaged in sex education.

Willem Van der Marck, O.P. "Vruchtbaarheidsregeling: poging tot antwoord op een nog open vraag." *Tijdschrift voor Theologie*, 1963, pp. 386-413.

Defends the moral liceity of "the pill" on the basis of an analogy with the transplantation of organs.